dear dad,

it's over.

xoxo,

M Dickson

turning custody into candor

"every child loses something a whole life can't fulfill"

- sophie b. hawkins

dear dad, it's over.

M Dickson

ISBN: 978-1-936214-67-9
Library of Congress Control Number: 2011944574

Proofread by Karen Kibler.

Wyatt-MacKenzie Publishing
DEADWOOD, OREGON

Wyatt-MacKenzie Publishing, Inc, Deadwood, Oregon
www.WyattMacKenzie.com

for Nanny, who always had to have the last word

Maybe you could have done it differently
Maybe you could have left a little more love for me
And maybe you could have tried a little harder
To be a father – to a daughter

Because once upon a time –
So many stories ago
There was a child –
This little girl you used to know
And oh, she loved you –
She loved you to the moon
Yes, there was a little girl
But I guess I grew up too soon

○

I wrote that poem in bad cursive on the inside of my social studies notebook when I was fourteen years old. I had no idea yet how the years still to come would continue to tear me and my father apart. I didn't know yet that it would never really get any better. I also, apparently, didn't know how to pay attention in social studies class.

Dear Dad,

It's over. This tangled, tortuous thing that we have shared between us for all these twenty some odd years is done now. I am putting my foot down and I am walking away. You can take this as your Dear John letter. I have reached my breaking point and I am just so tired. I cannot break even one more time. My heart is covered over with band-aids and scars from all the times I should have called it quits. But better late than never I suppose, so I am doing it now. Enough is enough. You have disappointed me and as you have told me more than once, I have disappointed you. So, let's call it a draw. You can tell your friends this was mutual if it makes you feel any better.

I just do not want to feel the way that you can make me feel anymore. I don't even know how you do it. No one can ruin my day as fast as you can. Did you know that? Probably not. I would never tell you as much because I was always so afraid to let my guard down around you. I don't like the version of myself that I become where you're concerned. Sometimes I hardly recognize myself.

I feel as if I have chased your love but never caught it. I am so tired of running after you. If I have even a piece of it perhaps it is just better for me to give it away. I would hate to lose it.

This is not a fight so please do not mistake it for one. I am not seeking an apology and I would prefer that you not offer one. Besides, I would probably just assume you were doing it to ease your own conscience anyway. And that's the worst of kind of "I'm sorry." My decision is final. Please hear my words and know that I have wanted to say them for so very long. Know that I have bitten my tongue when I wanted to bite off your head, that I have caved to your pressure when it felt like the walls were caving in on me and that I have walked on egg shells while my heart was breaking.

Please don't think that I hate you. That would be terrible for my karma. I don't like you very much. I imagine that's probably fairly evident given the break up and all but just like Dolly said, I will always love you. You seem like you lead a happy life and I hope that's true. I want you to be happy. But I gotta be honest, more than that—I want for me to be happy. And I just don't think I can get there with you in my life anymore. So I am letting you off the hook. You will no longer be measured against my expectations of what a father should be because I will no longer expect anything from you. It is the only surefire way to make sure that you never again disappoint me.

It's not all bad when I look back so thank you for the good times and the sweet memories. I want you to know that the bad ones have stolen none of their nostalgia.

Now here is where I would tell you that I'm going to miss you but the truth is Dad, I already do. I have missed you for most of my life. I hope you will remember that if someday you should find yourself missing me.

> *Love,*
> *Your daughter*

Memories are like photographs. They are stamped not only with a date and time but imprinted forever with the feeling that they created. For good or for bad they are forever linked to an unshakable emotion.

As I wrote these words out on these pages I was not always able to speak with complete clarity about all the delicate details of each moment. My mind did not grant me a perfect recollection of each passing particular. I may not have been able to recall what time of year or the day of the week it was but I do know with perfect assurance just how each encounter and each exchange made me feel. These pages hold the phrases and the words that best articulate those intangible emotions as I felt them then and as I see them now. Some have come better into focus over the years and some still sit blurred behind nostalgia and far too often, tears.

It all began as a conversation within myself. It was a breaking down of sorts, an intimate interrogation. But I was asking questions of myself for which I did not know the answers. So what I had intended to be a simple exercise in self-exploration instead became a journey through my memories and that journey became this book.

I had reached a point in my life where I knew instinctively that the time had come to end my relationship with my father. With age had come wisdom and I now knew myself well enough to know that I did not possess the necessary skills and defenses to endure the continued drama and disappointments that our straining bond consistently provided. I knew that I was no longer capable of handling with any modicum of grace the various ups and downs that we so often battled. In truth, I realized that maybe I never had been. I knew that it was absolutely necessary for my own mental health and emotional well-being that I remove my father from my life in the same way that you remove any toxic relationship. I had to dump him. A break-up was in order. That would be the only way that I could take the next steps toward healing.

I knew all of these things to be true but I struggled some with the whys of it. It was hard to single out just which straw it was that drove this particular camel into the ground. I began to dig through the pictures of moments frozen in my mind and the reasons grew clearer as the proof shone through the pain. What I found hidden behind the should-have-beens and could-have-beens was the truth about what was and what wasn't.

It is important for you to know before you read even an inch farther that I am not angry. This is not about revenge and it is not about being mad. These broken pieces of my past are gone and I refuse to carry them around like some sort of Sherpa, hell-bent on setting off on mountains made of molehills. The anger has long subsided. But what has remained is the hurt. I have written these pages in an effort to relieve myself of that as well.

This is my story about my father. This is not a book about my mother's ex-husband or my grandmother's son. I have not painted a picture of good versus bad or right versus wrong because I know that my father is not a villain and that I am not a saint.

What I am is perhaps a childish twenty-six. I do not own a home and my mostly urban lifestyle requires no car. My artistic callings called for no college degree so I never bothered to obtain one. My friends are a motley crew with similar ambitions and equally-lacking academic achievements. I have no ring on my finger nor do I have the urgent desire to put one there. And through the grace of God and Trojan, I have no children. My bank account over the course of a fiscal year reads like the blueprint of a roller coaster and if before nightfall I've remembered to eat dinner—I count the day as a success. In this particular phase of my life I would be no one's perfect parent. I am selfish and career oriented. I am an arrogant overachiever.

It is armed with this perspective that I have tried to give my dad, a father by age twenty-three, the benefit of the doubt. But objective reasoning gives way to confusion; for it was never in these years, my early childhood, that he failed me. I have many early happy memories with my father that are just as vivid and haunting as the ones that were to come later in my life. It was he who helped teach me how to imagine and create. We would sit for hours making up songs on his guitar, writing stories on his old typewriter or battling Nerf sword to Nerf sword in epic pirate battles. He was the perfect playmate.

It was as he and I grew older that the distance grew wider. Both emotionally and geographically. The man who had walked me into my kindergarten class was nowhere to be found when I boarded the bus to first grade. He was not present at back-to-school conferences; he did not read report cards or help with science projects. He never knew my friends or my teachers. At times I have wondered if he has ever known me as more than the child with whom he once played.

Weekend visits were not accurate portrayals of my day-to-day life. My father never had to check my homework or monitor my curfew, he didn't assign me chores or dole out an allowance. My father picked me up long after school had ended on a Friday and brought me home before bedtime on Sunday. He was the perpetual playmate to an aging child.

I may be a childish twenty-six but I am an adult. And the person that I have become is a stranger to my father.

But, of course, before we discuss the now we must first discuss the then. Though by the time you read this the now will also be then but then I suppose that part isn't too important.

one.

My parents were in their early thirties when they divorced in February of 1992. I was six years old or, as I likely would have told you at the time, an elderly six and three-quarters. I was precocious and inquisitive, likely to be found rattling on about imaginary friends and fairy tales or holding court in a room full of Barbie dolls. But in February of 1992, I was the only child of a marriage that lasted just shy of eight years, the only bullet loaded in for that particular game of Russian roulette and the judges and lawyers were firing the gun.

It is a strange thing to be a child and to be told that your parents are divorcing. Until I heard the words from my mother's lips it had never crossed my young mind that the definition of the word family could be so easily changed.

Full physical custody was awarded to my mother,

and my father never contested it. In all my years he has never done anything else for which I am as grateful. A piece of paper with a signature I'll never recognize mandated that every other Friday and sometimes on holidays I would find myself clutching a small suitcase and journeying an hour or two from my home, my toys, and my mother. If these occasions made me feel anything but inconvenienced and lonely, I can't remember now.

My mother's family, which I have never referred to as anything more than mine, was loud and more alive than most. When we all crowded together, four walls could hardly contain us and we would often spill into cousins' backyards and onto aunts' kitchen tables. Laughter rang out loudly over lively conversations, debates heated up over coffee, and someone, somewhere, was always cooking something. When I recall my childhood it is these feelings frozen in time, these bits of family video that loop my mind, that are by far my favorite. So it was always with a heavy heart and a feeling of loss that I would climb into my father's car and take off up the highway for a weekend that I was sure could never equal the one that I was missing.

The ink had barely dried on the divorce papers before my father had moved the last of his things into the home of his former mistress-turned-girlfriend. Together they shared her stiff, child-fearing townhouse and for two weekends a month I lived out of a suitcase in the guest room. They tried, often too hard, to make me feel welcome and keep me entertained but the rules were different, the house was cold and the food tasted funny. Sunday could never come quickly enough.

It was hard to adjust to being split in two and I didn't always do it well. There were nights when I was scolded for crying or for missing my mother. I was not allowed to say out loud that all I wanted was to go home. I was made to feel guilty that my honest emotional distress made my father feel inadequate. The subject of whether or not he really was inadequate was never open for discussion.

Even now as I write this I am consumed with the familiar feeling of guilt. Ridiculous. In spite of every tie that I have severed, I just cannot shake the instinct to protect my father's feelings. But as I discovered recently, there is a reason for that that goes far beyond common courtesy or family values. See, I have a mouth on me. I know this. As a child, and certainly as a teenager, I was rarely reprimanded for what I said and instead for the way I said it. My emotions, when left unguarded, would fly out of me in caustic tones. My voice would get raised, my aim got sharpened. I kept an eye on the jugular and I rarely missed a shot. It was for this reason that my mother and I often found ourselves at odds as I aged. We fought frequently. There would be quiet bickering laced with sarcasm and subtly or all-out word wars. We would stand toe to toe shouting to be heard over each other for varying lengths of time until she had put me back in my place, and that is just the way that adolescence goes. I would test my boundaries and find my voice with my mother because I knew that even if she played the enemy she was, in fact, the safety net. No matter how long an argument would last, once it had come to some sort of reasonable conclusion, it was done. Vanished. Our relationship would resume again just as strong as it had ever been. I know it drove my mother crazy that I never felt the same freedom of speech with my father.

My dad has over the years hurt me more times than I can count. I would often feel slighted by what he did not do and let down by what he did. For years I felt like my father regarded every emotion I managed to communicate as suspicious. As if the feelings weren't truly mine and I had, instead, just been sent on a mission to manipulate him courtesy of my mother. That was never true, of course, and the moments of doubt that passed between us often made me feel like a common criminal. If I tried to swap a weekend so I could attend the birthday party of a friend from school he saw it only as my mother getting extra time. When my grandparents wanted to treat me to Christmas in Disney World my father wrote my mother a three-page-long letter telling her how awful she was for taking me away. There was never a mention that it might come to be one of my favorite childhood memories or what a special expe-rience it might be for me. My father always treated me like an extension of my mother and rarely of himself.

But I cannot in all good conscience put all of the

blame on him that the rifts grew wider. I know that of all the times my father has hurt me, he probably knows of very few. I could never properly verbalize those feelings with him in the same way that I could with my mother. Sometimes it was because I did not want to appear affected. I did not feel like he deserved to know that he could have such an impact on me. I did not want to look overly weak or sensitive. I was afraid to be vulnerable or to show that I cared. But more often than not, when I look back now with a calmer mind and the benefit of age, I realize that I was not just protecting myself. I was working, despite anything my father did, to keep our relationship in the best possible condition. Because his love never felt unconditional. So I flinch a little inside with each emotion that I commit to paper because I know that I am also committing to the consequences of my words and the condition in which my father might find his love ....

"...that feeling of safety you prize
well, it comes with a hard, hard price
you can't shut off the risk and pain
without losin' the love that remains"

- bruce springsteen

two.

The first time I met my father's wife she was my father's boss.

It was a midsummer picnic on their company's dime and though my parents were still married my mother had opted to miss the festivities. She cited a headache as the reason. Whether she already had one or was sure the chain of events would lead to one is unclear now. Three cheers for foresight.

I cannot remember the exact moment that the introduction took place. I barely remember the day. But I do remember a water balloon fight that lit up my five-year-old face. My partner in aqua warfare was a seemingly sweet woman in her early thirties who let me lead the way and kept my stockpile of balloons fully loaded. Later I would gush to my mother over the new friend that I had made at the picnic. I rambled on and on, all about how much fun we had had together.

I am sure that I, like most excitable children, repeated the epic battle story over and over again in the days that followed. I can only imagine how many times and ways I filled my mother's ears with childlike wonder over my new partner in crime.

It would be years before I would come to understand the significance of that meeting. Would be years before I would realize that the woman who had so enthusiastically played with me that day was playing more adult games with my married father on a regular basis. Years before I would truly understand the sheer audacity and disrespect that my father had displayed that day.

In truth, the details of my father's adultery are really none of my business. I have always assumed that cheating is the product of an unhappy relationship and not the cause of it. I imagine my parents were hardly the exception to this rule. What I take from this memory is not my father's glaring lack of a moral compass, but instead in it I see the first instance of what would ultimately cause our demise. I believe that no relationship, be it a marriage or otherwise, can survive without respect. In this interaction and in so many more over the years, my father continued to show me that he was a man who possessed very little of it for others and in turn, was perhaps worthy of even less.

When my father took me out to dinner to celebrate my seventh birthday, just a month after the divorce was finalized, his girlfriend came along. Two years later she was his pregnant wife. My father wasted no time building his new family as I struggled to find my footing in the broken foundation of the first. I never had a single father.

three.

Now I will say nothing more on the subject of my father's wife, until I first state with all sincerity that in many ways she is a better person than I am. It's very likely that she is even a better person than you are. I say that without a hint of humor or the slightest wink. Seriously. My stepmother is an endlessly generous, sweet and well-meaning woman. I believe whole-heartedly that if it had not been for her influence over the years, my father would have let our strained relationship slip away a long time ago. And though her devoted Christian ways made a believer out of her once atheist husband, there were times over the years I wished more than anything that she would just cinch her Bible-belt tight enough to keep her mouth shut.

The woman always wanted to talk. She had an irrelevant answer for everything and often tried to identify with me as a "child of divorce." Her folks split when she was an adult, she had two full siblings and neither of her parents went on to have any more children. I was able to call bullshit on her attempts at relating even at an early age. But in the interest of being fair, I must admit that there probably was not much of anything that she could have said that would have conjured up any feeling in me besides resentment. Each word she offered or effort she made was one more stabbing reminder that my father wasn't making a sound.

His silence was never louder than it was when the topic of faith rolled into the conversation. My mother's family has always been implicitly religious. I was raised to attend church every Sunday and kneel for my prayers every night. After my parents divorced my grandmother was certain that each Sabbath that I spent away from home and at my father's was slowly chipping away at pieces of my soul. Hyperbole is right at home in Catholicism. But, in her defense, I was young and impressionable for sure. I was a child taking my first steps in building a life of faith and my stepmother was consistently vocal about her deep-seated disapproval. While she was once a Catholic herself she, like so many others, had grown to dislike the church and instead chose to hop from one Christian outpost to another, picking up the bits that she liked along the way and leaving the rest behind. I was often told by her how wrong my mother's chosen denomination was and was made to attend alternative church services. In snarky tones, but with some accuracy, my grandmother would often remark that my father's wife was a member of the Church of What's Happening Now.

Without any faith of his own, my father followed blindly behind her and dragged me right along with him. I quickly came to dread those spirituality infused hours in unfamiliar settings because they made me feel endlessly uncomfortable. I was only eight years old the first time of many times that my stepmother told me her thoughts on the Catholic Church. I was just a child and having my beliefs called into question so often made me feel demeaned and embarrassed. I was precocious, but my faith was precarious.

Regardless of what one believes about God or about religion I believe that it is undoubtedly evident that it was never my stepmother's place to intrude on the spiritual upbringing that had been set into motion by my actual mother. When I look back now on the things she said and the way that she said them, I cannot imagine her ever speaking to her daughters in such a manner. I cannot imagine that she would ever want anyone to speak to them that way. But my father never said a word.

He never once made it necessary for her to separate the man who she married from the man who was my father. But to me the distinction was always clear. Perhaps it was petty and immature, the result of a suppressed desire to stomp my feet and exclaim *"I was here first. He's mine!"* but I grew in many ways to dislike his wife. I know now that it was not for who she was but for what she so clearly represented. She was my father's first choice. When my parents divorced my father didn't just leave my mother for another woman, he left me. He took his clothes and his guitar, he packed up his books and his records and he moved to a new town to start a new life. Weekends spent with him and with her became painful reminders that my father knew that I could not move seamlessly with him into his new life and that it hadn't much mattered at all.

Time spent alone with him quickly became limited to however long it took him to drive us from my house to theirs on Friday and back again on Sunday. Weekends with him came to mean weekends with his wife and her family. Sometimes I was grateful for the distraction, but more often than not the gatherings of aunts, uncles and cousins found me longing for my own. I barely felt at home amongst my father's family and I certainly felt alone in a crowd of his in-laws.

It was a swift and jarring transition. I had hardly yet come to terms with the idea that my father and my mother together no longer represented any applicable meaning of family and suddenly I was swimming in a sea of strangers.

four.

It is worth noting, in the interest of context, that my father's family could never be mistaken for The Waltons or any more relevant, equally stable nuclear unit. Somewhere around the fall of '73 my paternal grandfather went out for a pack of cigarettes and never seemed to find his way home. My grandmother, an otherwise mostly sane woman, still hangs their wedding picture in her bedroom as though she believes he might stumble in one night complaining about thirty-some odd years of traffic. For this reason, or perhaps a thousand others, my father has never truly understood the depth of family ties.

His emotionally distant Irish kin were the perfect foil to my mother's close knit Italian clan. What served as conversation at one dinner table would be thought of as banal small talk at the other. This distinction was never clearer than at the holidays. If I thought I was missing out on family fun on the weekends, I knew it for sure on Holy Days and other annual celebrations. But it was a Thanksgiving Day in the early nineties, when I couldn't have been more than seven, that has stayed with me far past its welcome. I can still remember the fear that I felt in me as clearly as if it all had happened just yesterday.

Thanksgiving with my mother's family was an epic event. Just the anticipation of it made getting through Wednesday's school day a difficult task every year. I knew for sure that once the holiday was underway I would be surrounded by numerous aunts, uncles and cousins. My grandmother was one of six sisters, each of whom had married and had their own children and for the most part those children had gone on to have children of their own. And no one missed Thanksgiving. A typical year found sixty to seventy people gathered under one roof to give thanks for good food and each other. If I had a time machine, these are the days for which I would travel.

It had been decided that on this particular Thanksgiving my father would come and whisk me away just after dinner for a weekend to be spent at a hotel in the mountains with him, his not-yet wife and a few of their friends. I can still remember the sinking feeling I had in my stomach as I watched the clock count down the hours. To a child a year might as well be a decade. How could I miss out on those last precious hours of Thanksgiving when the next one was so very far away? Still, I had already learned by then that the post-divorce he said/she said (mostly he said) carried more weight than my high hopes for an unshared holiday. So I sat upstairs, suitcase packed, coat on, waiting, while the sounds of my cousins still playing and laughing drifted up from the basement. My mother made several futile attempts to cheer me up. She offered promises that I'd have fun once I got there and reminded me over and over again that I'd see everyone again soon enough. In retrospect, I realize now that those holiday separations were just as hard on her as they were on me but at the time, she was equally the villain. She was practically pushing me out the door and insisting that I go ... so off I went.

My father and I made it a few miles up the highway, maybe half an hour or so, before my stiff upper lip began to quiver and soon enough I was crying. I had tried to put on a brave face. I had tried not to make my father feel bad but I desperately wanted to turn around. I wanted something familiar. I wanted my family. I did not want to be in a car with a man who barely knew me, racing away from home to see people I didn't know do things I didn't care about. Unfortunately, at that time my father was not a man with a lot of empathy. He yelled at me. I had never seen him that angry. He spat his words at me saying that it was his time now and he would not give me back to my mother, he called me selfish and inconsiderate. I had never in my life been talked to like that. Like I was just a possession to be owned. He spoke as if I was something that could be divided up into pieces. I sobbed harder and he screamed louder. He became so frustrated with me that he spun the car around in the middle of the Garden State Parkway, driving in the opposite direction of traffic for a moment, as if that were the way to take me home, before spinning it back around and reminding me that this was his weekend. I was terrified. The man who was supposed to be protecting me was growing manic before my eyes. Finally, he pulled the car over on the shoulder of the road beside a pay phone. He called my mother, demanding that she come get me, then he opened the car door to tell me that he was so furious that he couldn't even stand to be in the car with me. I will never in my life for as long as I live forget the moment that my father looked me in the eye and told me that I made him sick. He spat the words out at me and then slammed the door shut. I waited alone in the dark for my mother to come and save me.

To this day my father and I have never spoken of that night. I am certain that he must remember it but I doubt if that memory carries with it any weight. To him it was a detour on the highway, a delay in his ski trip and a temporary bruise on his ego. I, however, was more permanently wounded.

But that was not the first time that my father failed to realize the lasting impact of his fleeting impulses.

When my parents were still married, in what I suppose would have been called the early years had there been any later ones, my father allowed his job to transfer him out of New Jersey and into Massachu-setts. I will note that I am hesitant to write about this period of time because I do not remember it all that well. I was just four years old and the consequences of this geographical blunder would not impact me for years. These days, when asked, my mother speaks in sour tones about the year we spent living in New England and my father has rarely spoken of it at all. I have come to understand that this time proved to be pivotal in the chain of events that would lead to my parents' divorce but that is knowledge I acquired later and it has no place here. The story I wish to tell is of a small and seemingly insignificant event that is now so startlingly symbolic it is almost laughable. It is also one of the few perfectly clear memories that I have from that time.

It was a rare night out for my then stay-at-home mom who had chosen to accompany a neighbor to a local Chinese auction. My father was tasked with watching me and as I have said previously and most willingly, he was often an ideal playmate. Like most children I was enamored with entering the world of make believe, and he was a solid companion with which to travel. On that particular evening a pirate was my character of choice and an epic battle ensued in the dining room of our second floor apartment. Like any good pirate stepping into a duel, I needed a sword. For lack of a prop closet, I grabbed a nearby broom and my dad laughed at the resourcefulness I displayed. The game went on just fine for a moment or two until the object slipped from my hand and the stick collided with my father's face. He yelled out in surprise then grabbed me swiftly, striking me hard with his hand in one rash and angry movement.

I was stunned. My father had never done anything like that before. My parents did not regard hitting as an acceptable form of discipline and it was certainly off the table as a knee jerk reaction. Tears rushed down my face as I raced to the telephone. My clumsy fingers pounded out a familiar number and I cried to myself until I heard my grandmother, my mother's mother, come on the other end of the line. I was four years old but I knew enough to know that my father had done something wrong. More than hitting me, he had terrified me. He had violently overreacted when accidentally injured by a child during a children's game. I remember him taking the phone away from me and speaking quietly with my grandmother. He was sheepish and apologetic. The rest of the evening doesn't exist in the scrapbook of mind and so I can only assume that it was, at least comparatively, uneventful.

Now, that story has been recounted several times over the years by both sides of my family as a humorous anecdote. I was the brazen little girl who told on her daddy. But to me that single moment in time represents something far more meaningful than that. I was a child battling with an adult and when my innocent actions caused me to accidentally hurt my father he did not react as my protector or my parent but instead as an immature peer. That night was the first of many battles my father and I would wage but it would hardly be the last time that he fought me like a child.

It is not lost on me, nor should it be on you, that in a heated moment with my father I had sought comfort in my grandmother. Over the years I would turn to my mother's sisters and aunts and cousins in much the same way. It was an instinct that my father resented in my mother and one that he eventually came to resent in me, too.

five.

Not very long after what will henceforth be referred to as "the great and awful Thanksgiving incident" my mother, well technically I, took my father to court in an effort to help insure that nothing like that ever happened again. At the time, and perhaps even now, I was the youngest person on record in the state of New Jersey to do such a thing. I suppose that something like that would be an impressive achievement if the implication wasn't such a depressing footnote.

For some time, even before the great and awful Thanksgiving incident, my father had been pressing my mother for a more structured visitation schedule where the holidays were concerned. It was an idea that did not sit well with her in light of less-than-favorable turkey-related events and the fact that his family really had no traditions of which to speak.

It was obvious by then that it was more than likely that a holiday away from my family would come to mean a holiday with my father's future in-laws and without a paternal relative in sight. When my mother approached her lawyer about my father's request to alter the terms of the visitation agreement she was advised that the best chance for getting a favorable outcome would be if it were I, and not she, who counter-sued him. And so was born Baby's First Legal Brief.

There was no state precedent yet set for such a thing and the judge presiding over the case was understandably hesitant to dictate a parent's rights based on what could have been a child's whim. So I, the adorable plaintiff, was made to meet with him one-on-one so that he could better ascertain my level of maturity. The privacy of his chambers also served a dual purpose in that neither my mother nor my father would be a witness to my testimony.

I can still clearly remember sitting anxiously, my feet dangling as I tried to keep my best posture in an oversized leather chair. I wonder now if I looked as important as I felt. Just a few weeks earlier I had made my first confession to a priest and I remember thinking that it felt somewhat the same. I knew that the emphasis on the truth was of equal importance in both scenarios and so I told it as best I could. If I was supposed to be intimidated, I hadn't known it.

The older man listened sympathetically with an earnest ear as I explained my emotions and worked to keep my tears at bay. I tried hard to convey clearly the feelings that even I could not yet fully understand. We talked as the clock ticked on for well past an hour. When we were finished, the judge returned to the courtroom and I to my mother. Later he would tell her that I was a sweet and articulate child. Then he would sign a paper that said I never had to go with my dad for another Thanksgiving Day.

It was the first time that I had to oppose my father in court but it would certainly not be the last. Such things are sadly almost a rite of passage when you are a child of divorce. Victories in court can come to mean so much more to a child who has had legal restraints imposed upon them since the time their parents decided that their binding legal agreement was void. I could do nothing to stop the fact that custody controlled my life, but that day in court taught me a lesson which I did not soon forget. I was a whole person no matter how they tried to split me and my small voice was worthy of being heard.

six.

My great grandmother passed away the summer after my parents divorced. I was seven and it was the first time I was dealing with a loss of that magnitude. My Nonnie had been an integral part of my family for all my life and I struggled with understanding death and saying good-bye. After all, it was she who had taught me to tie my shoes and to color in between the lines. When you're a child, those are practically the keys to the universe. I found myself discovering a new kind of sadness and I alternated between acknowledging it and abruptly tossing it aside in favor of a new toy or game. Such are the perks of being a kid.

I would go on to attend the funeral with my mother but she did not think that it was necessary for me, at such a young age, to be present for all the hours of a wake so she asked my father to look after me while she attended the services. I remember sitting in the backseat of his little red car as we drove with his girl-friend, who used to be his mistress but was not yet his wife, to a picnic area down by the bay beach where a barbecue was taking place. I cannot remember the exact occasion for the outing, but it was summer in a beach town and often that is reason enough for such an event. Some members of my father's family were going to be in attendance and my mother thought it would be a good distraction for me given the circum-stances. I ended up distracted all right, but not in the way she had intended. Of course, the day probably would have rolled along just fine if it hadn't been for something I said.

We were almost there. I could smell the water. The cement street was slowly giving way to the dirt road that would lead us to our destination when my father began to rattle off the names of who we might see that day. At the time, my mother's first cousin was dating a longtime friend of my dad's and he mentioned during the duration of his list that they would be there together. I was relieved. I felt immediate comfort in knowing that if I got that strange sort of sad again at least someone would be there who would under-stand. Someone else who knew my great grand-mother and who was missing her, just like me. I remarked with palpable relief and a child's innocence,

"Oh, good. Someone from my family will be there!"

The air in the car froze in an instant. It was the very worst thing that I could have said. My father snapped at me with a raised voice. In a harsh tone he told me that he knew that I had never thought of his family as my own and that I had always favored my mother's side. Never? Always? When I think about this now I wish more than anything that I had had the foresight to yell back at him, "*I'm seven! How the hell long could always be?*" but I suppose that wouldn't have helped the matter much. Instead I sat quietly in my seat as he berated me. I felt my face grow red with embarrassment and a sick, guilty feeling shook my stomach. I remember wishing that his girlfriend wasn't there. I remember wishing I wasn't there. I felt humiliated. I had not consciously intended to make that distinction and I certainly had not meant to verbally antagonize my father.

But his defenses had been riled, his insecurities highlighted. If he had paused for just a moment, if he had given it just a second thought before lashing out at me, maybe he would have realized then what I have come to realize now. Those words, that "always" and that "never," they were not intended for me. They were the cliff notes of a war waged between my parents. The lexicon of long showdowns between his and her holidays and family obligations. I was just a child, who in my eagerness, had simply misspoke. I was his child. But when my father looked in the rear view mirror that afternoon he did not see in me any

part that could have been a reflection of himself.
Instead, I believe, he saw only my mother.

seven.

I must ask that you allow me some leeway as I begin this next chapter. You will have to pardon me because there is no appropriate literary segue for this next particular bit of information. Probably because the whole thing was just so damn out of the blue to begin with. What, at the time, seemed only slightly odd now, in retrospect and written here, seems extraordinarily ridiculous.

My father and his not-yet-at-that-time wife were, I can only assume, bored. That is the only slightly logical explanation that I can possibly put together for why they would decide one summer to open up their home, that child-fearing townhouse complete with the all too familiar guest room, to a child from Ireland. Are you reading this right? They decided to import in a kid with a perfectly good family back home to America for a six-week stint in the States.

Perhaps it is just not as much fun to parent your own child as it is to foster a rental. Maybe they just wanted to play house. Who the hell knows.

Either way, I was eight and excited, and it would be years before this all seemed so outlandish. Mostly I was just looking forward to a new friend and the distraction she would create. They told me at first that she was eight just like me. But I remember glancing at the paperwork with my father's girlfriend one day when I noticed the date of birth on the girl's form. My math skills are hardly genius but I had subtraction down to a science even then. She was eleven, nearly twelve. When I made note of my discovery out loud I was patronized with a *"Well, aren't you smart"* and placated with a reassurance that a child from a foreign country would really act much closer to my age than I might expect. Even then it seemed like such a silly, trivial thing to lie to me about but it was hardly the last of the deceit that situation would bring.

The child came to them via a program based in Northern Ireland. It had religious roots and placed a strong emphasis on family values and so it was insistent that all of the children involved be placed in a happy home where the guardians were married. I was instructed that if asked, I needed to lie. I was to say that my father and his girlfriend were in fact, husband and wife. It was a strenuous task to give to a young child and I was often fearful that I would slip up but I never did. Though once while the little girl lay sleeping upstairs I was called into the kitchen and interrogated. While I was between visits and home at my mother's she had been asking to see wedding pictures and my father's girlfriend found it to be a suspicious line of questioning. I told her then, as I tell you now, that I hadn't said a word. I imagine that, like many young girls, our Irish import was enamored with the idea of a wedding's pomp and circumstance and just wanted to indulge in an afternoon of pretty pictures. But I knew that my denial was not believed.

My father had requested that in the custody agreement it be stipulated that during the summer, in addition to the regular every other weekend routine that I loved so much, I was to spend two consecutive weeks at his house. So that summer I left my beachfront hometown and headed north. Both he and his make-believe wife worked real full-time jobs so my days were spent with my foreign friend at a day camp which I quickly came to loathe. At home I had been being cared for by my family during the day while my mother worked but with my father I found myself being looked after by strangers clocking in for minimum wage. To make it all a little worse, the age difference between myself and the girl was never more apparent than when we were around other children. Her group of friends was older and by that definition alone they were cooler. Any attempts I made to socialize with her at the camp were met with taunts and giggles. Some even went so far as to accessorize the laughs with finger-points and eye-rolls.

When in the company of others, I was treated like an annoying kid sister.

One night during my two-week stay, a careless plating of cookies and milk left me with a bellyful of sour dairy product. I threw up everywhere the next morning and so I was granted a reluctant reprieve from a day of enforced recreation. If I could have given a high five to my sensitive stomach, I would have slapped it silly.

Each time I visited that summer, we shared the guest room. But I slept on the trundle bed now. I tagged along on beach trips and to ball games but I wasn't invited when they took her to Disney World. The temporary stand-in kid had somehow nudged me out of the benefits of a more permanent position. I know now that what I had originally thought would be fun months of memories was actually a six-week window into the future.

eight.

January of 1995 has no place in a history book. For most, it was a cold and uneventful month filled with post-holiday stress and snow showers. An unremarkable collection of days and nights. But for me it brought an irreversible shift in my ever-changing life. At 6:03 pm on the last day of the year's first month my father's wife gave birth to a baby girl. Suddenly I was no longer my father's only child. I was simply his first try. I had firmly become the remainder from the division of his first attempt at a family. He, his wife and new baby made up the perfect picture, and on occasion I was required to hang onto the frame and smile.

I remember counting down the months leading up to my sister's arrival. I would bow my head and include her in my prayers every night.

"Dear God, please let the baby be healthy. Dear God, please let it be a girl."

I was nine and nervous. I was afraid that my step-mother was going to deliver a baby boy. I had lost so much of my father's attention already and I was certain that a son would be enough to distract him forever. It wasn't logical or reasonable but it was scary and I was nine.

It is certainly a common enough occurrence for an older child to feel apprehensive or even jealous at the thought of a new baby. Some children find it diffi-cult to digest the idea of having to change their world to accommodate a sibling. But I was not one of those children. I wasn't worried about sharing my world; I was only scared that my father's would be more fully consumed.

Another baby came along in June of 1998 and brought with her new emotions for me to carry. My two half sisters were each other's whole and suddenly the space between us felt much further apart than the branches of a family tree.

My mother's sister had had a son out of wedlock a few years before I came along. His dad disappeared soon after my aunt became pregnant and my cousin has never met his father. There were times when I was envious of this. I often imagined that by having no father at all my cousin was spared the heartache of having one that continually fell short of his expectations. The great let-down, the prevailing disappointment, was stagnant. He grew up and he got over it. My father left but he lingered. Each new interaction we shared brought with it a chance for me to be let down all over again. My cousin never had to wonder if his would have been a good dad. All evidence points to the contrary. But when my father had other children I learned the hardest truth. He was capable of being an excellent father. He just wasn't going to be one to me.

There are many differences between a full sibling and a half sibling, the least of which are biological. If my father had never had another child I would have been left to imagine what a life with him could have been like. I could have been free to wax poetic about maybes and might haves. Instead I watched him parent as though it was a spectator sport, and I admit that there were times when I was guilty of keeping score.

My one father has three daughters. But I will get no second attempt. I will have no third try. A parent has the freedom and often the ability to have as many children as they please and with every one, a fresh start; but a child will only ever have one experience, one permanent biological bond and the imprints inflicted from those interactions are not so easily wiped clean.

Somewhere, sometime ago after one too many beers my father told me that he often worried that I believed he loved my sisters more than he loved me. I told him he was wrong but in truth, I struggle with this still. In all my twenty-six years I have never once doubted that on some level my father loved me. I know to my core that he would step in front of a bullet to protect me, give his last breath to save me, and demonstrate a variety of other hyperbolic gestures. But I have never believed, not for a moment, that he liked me. His love never felt unconditional or emotional; rather it felt obligatory and assumed. It felt like it could be taken away at any moment much like he himself was removed. I cannot envision him ever leaving my sisters in the way that he left me, so perhaps by that definition yes, I do believe that he loves them more. But I cannot put it into concrete terms because it feels too fragile. As if by speaking it I might somehow will it to be true if it wasn't already.

I am the product of my mother's presence and my father's absence. I represent none of his ideals or values because he was not there to instill them. I am no reflection of my father on any surface deeper than a mirror. We share no common bonds beyond biology. I visited my father's house, and my sisters were raised in his home, and that has been the greatest difference.

When you are an adult, comfort is a luxury; but when you are a child it is a greatly craved stabilizing force. It's less about back rubs and more about backbone. For ten years of my life, for two weekends each month, I was uncomfortable.

Every Friday afternoon I would pack up my belongings for a weekend away. And even though I was a child who so loved playing make-believe it was hard to convince myself that I was just heading over to my second home when each time it required luggage. When I was very young, just eight or nine at the most, my mother suggested to my father that perhaps if a suitcase wasn't necessary, if I had some clothes or toys at his house, maybe I wouldn't feel so much like a tourist. At this, my gainfully employed father went out and picked up some clothes from the Salvation Army, and stored them in a dresser in the spare room of his girlfriend's place. His misguided, half-assed attempt to make me feel comfortable was offering me the option of wearing someone else's clothes in someone else's house. I already felt like enough of a stranger, dressing like one hardly seemed to be the solution. So for ten years I carried a suitcase.

After the eldest of my younger sisters was born, my father and his wife bought a home on a pictur-esque street in a quaint suburban town an hour or so north of where I was growing up. It was a four-bedroom house. One for my father and his wife, one for the new baby, one for the exotic au pair that lived downstairs and a room where I slept. It was at least twice as big as the one before and it felt all that more empty. No attempt to decorate had been made and the bins and bags that lined the walls made it feel like an afterthought. I was a guest in a guest room and it never felt like anything more. When the next baby came along, the older of the two moved into the larger space and her old room became a nursery. A futon bed in the attic with my suitcase beside it was where I would serve out the remainder of my weekend obli-gations. Uncomfortably.

nine.

Now, I want to be the most clear about one thing because it would break my heart to have it be misunderstood. I love my sisters. I have never once, not even for the briefest of moments, encountered inside myself anything but love for them. If I have ever felt slighted or angry about circumstances stemming from their existence it was never an emotion that was consciously directed at them. My relationships with the girls have always felt, thankfully, distinctly different from my relationship with my father. I fear though, that as I separate myself from him, I will sadly lose them as well. And it, to a point, is somewhat understandable. I recognize that it may be hard for them to see things from my point of view when the father that they have always known has been so vastly different than the one I have described here on these pages.

I remember once, in a fit of preteen emo angst, the older of my younger sisters emailed me, berating me for not visiting as often as she would have liked. I had missed a birthday of my father's and it blew her young mind that I could do such a thing. I didn't tell her that I couldn't remember the last time I had gotten so much as a card from my dad on my birthday, let alone a visit, or that he, himself, hadn't invited me up for celebrations. When I replied saying that I simply hadn't had the money to make the trip she was quick to point out that she was positive that if I just asked him, her dad would have gladly funded my travel expenses. Yes, I was sure her dad would have but I wasn't sure mine would have done the same. We have known two different men. But this is her luck and my loss. I have never, not even slightly, wanted for my opinion of him to ever color her world.

I heard recently that for a school project she lauded my father as her ultimate hero. She's sixteen now. By the time I had reached sixteen I would have used a variety of words to describe my dad but "hero" would never have graced such a list. But her admiration is genuine and he has earned it.

It might take careful thought but I believe that either of my sisters, if pressed, can probably tell you with certainty how many nights of their lives have been spent away from my father. They have never known a holiday without him or imagined a picture of their family which would not prominently include him. He has been a constant to them and a fickle variable to me. He has been their team's coach and their dances' chaperon. He has signed every permission slip and endured every bellyache and fever. And for so long, I could not properly articulate the feelings these little facts could drudge up in me.

Too often I confused them with envy, which I was quick to suppress. My pride would never let me admit to such an insecure emotion. Imagine my relief when after some time and some thought I came to understand that it was just good ol' fashioned indignation. I wasn't upset that my sister had inquired about my whereabouts on our father's birthday or had from time to time questioned my loyalties. I was livid that she, a child born nearly ten years after me, thought she had to tell me when my father's birthday was or felt entitled enough to let me know what level of familial obligation she thought our relationship entailed. I was around long before she showed up, so how was I so quickly bumped out of the chain of command? It felt like an intern had come into my job and fired me. I wanted to lash out with things like *"Who do you think you are?"* and *"Are you kidding me right now?"* but I never did. The closest I came was a heated reply I shot off after receiving a particularly line-crossing email. I ,without much thought, told her in no uncertain terms that my relationship with my father was not something that she understood fully or had any right to discuss. I felt justified in doing it at the time, but I now wonder if it was just one more time that a lack of explanation left me looking like the bad guy.

From the time that she was born and through most of her early years of life I was a steady fixture. Until I was eighteen or so I would step into my role of big sister with great pride each Friday night and each Sunday good-bye that I gave promised a quick return. I loved her then just as I do now, fiercely in the protective sort of way that only a sister can. But I fear now that those protective instincts have in time backfired in a way that I will forever regret. In retrospect I have come to realize now that in my well-intentioned attempts to keep my father's image intact, perhaps I damaged mine instead. I know that my sister struggled when my regular weekend visits transitioned into less frequent sojourns. She was unaware of the details of the tumultuous relationship I was battling or the custodial strings that had held me in place. So I know that it was hard for her to reconcile in her mind why it was that I had taken to coming around less and less over the years. But I never felt like it was my place to discuss her father any more than it was her place to discuss mine. And so I pulled away again and again without much commentary. I left her to wonder. It made me feel as if I was no better than my father, and right or wrong, I resented him for putting me in such a position. I felt burdened under the weight of the imposed obligations.

Once after one too many virtual envelopes had come cascading into my inbox, I broke down and tried to consult with my father for some guidance on the delicate situation. In a message dated February 24th, 2008 I wrote:

"Hey Dad -

I don't know if (insert name here!) has mentioned at all the emails she has been sending me but I am really at a loss as to what to do next. She's constantly sending me messages telling me that she wishes she could see me more and she feels like I don't care or asking me questions about if you & my mom getting divorced has upset me so much that I'm scarred from it—it's getting to be a little much. I've explained several times now that I wish I could see her more, too but that's just not the way the situation is right now. I thought that by being there for her birthday and making an effort to email back and forth and always reply to text messages and stuff—I thought she would be able to see that I'm trying but I feel like we're just running in circles and she's still getting upset. If I call her she never has anything to say so we end up hanging up after a minute or two...and then I get emails asking me questions like am I scarred for life and telling me I need to get closer to God...

I know she must understand on a logical level that I'm not 15 anymore and I can't be coming every other weekend...but I still feel like I'm not getting through to her—and she's very emotional about it and I don't want to upset her but like I said...I'm at a loss for what to do. I get like 2 to 3 emails a week from her about this and I try to respond the best I can but yeah—I'm at a loss....

Maybe you can try to talk to her and see if there's some deeper issue going on or something? Or maybe you can just shed a little light for me on how I can get through to her better? I've tried to explain that I do wish I could spend more time with her but I live over an hour away, I don't have a car and I have a very busy work schedule—and if I had the opportunity to be there I would and that I love her and don't want her to be upset….but she keeps emailing about it and I don't know what else I can say to her…"

More than a month went by before my father finally took the time to write back:

"Very sorry for the late reply …

I guess, at the end of the day, it's nice to have someone who cares about you so much. She's 13 and is learning to communicate her feelings, which is a good thing. Admittedly, there may be a learning curve, but I think her intents are good … She loves you and wants you to be a bigger part of her life.

How was your Easter?"

…I had reached out for insight and instead he just handed me more irritation.

My father had broken free of his first family and tangled me up in his second. Sometimes I just wanted to be selfish. I wanted so badly to be as selfish as he had been. But I could never be so cold. My heart does not have an on and off switch the way his always seemed to. I guess that sort of thing isn't genetic. So instead I coddled and I sugarcoated. With each holiday still comes questions that I dodge and conflicting plans that I invent. I have no neat wrap-up for this soliloquy. I have not yet encountered the epiphany that will free me of this web that's been created but I lay here in wait. Whether I am the spider or the fly has yet to be seen.

ten.

Stephen Sondheim once wrote out a message so simple but much too often forgotten.

"Children will listen. Careful before you say, listen to me. Children will listen."

There are no moments of life which are truly without meaning. Even those that seem the smallest can, inside them, hold the heaviest of weights. Every moment is capable of carrying with it the most lasting of impacts. This is particularly true of any moment that includes a child.

My dad plays the guitar. He has played it for my whole life and he started many years before I ever came along. I will not use this space to knock my father's outward appearance or his somewhat lacking good looks. I will just say that if you saw him and my mother together you would agree almost immediately that yes, he must have played guitar. Whatever sort of understanding you come to infer from that is your own doing.

When I was very young everything about his playing fascinated me. I remember clearly the way his case looked, open on the floor in the den in our very first house. I would play with the felt lining and the buckles, always being so careful not to tear the stickers or break the strings. I would wait for him to come home and then I would sit beside him as he played, singing along to me all the while. When I had had enough of his divided attention I would wrap my small hands around the neck of the guitar to bring him back to me. Of course, I would never dream of stopping him when he played the song that he always said he had picked out just for me. The tune was mostly "Put It There" by Paul McCartney but where McCartney had penned "son" my father would sing "one" instead and smile at me over the instrument. They were private concerts and I was an enthralled and adoring fan of my rock star dad.

But the years went on and the guitar and its case, with its soft lining and shiny buckles, left my home right along with my father. He would still play some at his new house but not much for me anymore.

When the new babies came they both were given a song handpicked just for them, too. It was a special tradition to a man who so valued music. The first got a Jimmy Buffett classic and the second a church hymn that just seemed to fit.

One summer my court-appointed two-week stay overlapped my father's family vacation and so I had no choice but to accompany them to my stepmother's father's place down in North Carolina. Her dad and his wife were hospitable but I felt out of place.

The last night of our trip found us all seated on the back porch of the sprawling home while my father strummed his guitar for a captive audience. He narrated his song choices one by one. First he played the song for my sister, six years old and smiling, and then the one that been designated for the baby, barely three. She watched him attentively just as I once had. And then it came time for him to play my song and his fingers stumbled over the chords, his mouth mashed up the words. He would chuckle awkwardly and then try again. This went on for a moment or two until he just gave up. He had forgotten how to play it. He didn't remember my song.

The hot tears were sudden and they stung. I thanked God that it was dark outside and then I laughed and rolled my eyes in the way that a teenager will do when she wants you to think she doesn't care. My face flushed a deep red with embarrassment and I remember hoping that the hood of my sweatshirt obstructed everyone's view of my humiliation.

I had been waiting for my song. I had ascribed

so much meaning to those first memories of my father and I had foolishly believed they had meant something to him, too. But there in the porch light, on a lake in Carolina they, like the lyrics and the chords, had been forgotten.

eleven.

Beer is my father's drink of choice. Come to think of it I am not sure that I've ever even seen him partake in another category of adult beverage. I think it is safe to say that he prefers it not only to vodka but maybe even to water.

I am not an expert on alcoholism so I am in no position to cast aspersions. All I will say is that for much of his life, and nearly all of mine, he has consumed more booze than most. Just like his father and just like his mother. I don't say that to be cold or cutting; I say it because I have been raised to know since I was very young that addiction is something that permeates my family from both sides. I have lived my life on full alert of lingering vices.

I remember that it was in grade school after a particularly gruesome presentation about the dangers of drinking and driving that I began to fear traveling with my father. I became extremely wary of attending sporting events together or really any functions where I had to rely on my dad for safe transport. Was he drinking too much? How was I to know if an adult was intoxicated? My mind provided the voice-over to my real life after-school special. I expressed my concerns to my mother who told me to discuss my nervousness with my father. I'm sure she thought he would handle it calmly and soothe my worries. Instead he laughed at me and told me not to tell him what to do.

I have heard both of my sisters refer to beer as "evil" and they have for some time now. I know that they have complained quietly to some adults in our family that he drinks too much but it is not something anyone talks about. He's not a mean drunk. He cries and rambles on about the depth of his love the deeper he sinks into the bottle, but he doesn't get violent so the problem goes ignored. I remember once when the boy who lived next door joked one too many times about all the beer bottles in the recyclable bin. The way my father yelled at him was loud and unwar-ranted. I was embarrassed for the boy and I was embarrassed for my dad.

Each summer in my father's neighborhood the block shuts down for a party. Police barricades block off the ends of the street and the people pour out into them to celebrate the arrival of a new season. There are games and barbecue grills and there is of course, a copious amount of beer. The younger of my sisters was born in June and it just so happened that the day she was to come home from the hospital was the day of the annual block party event. What I remember most about that night is not what she wore or if she kept me up with her cries. What I do remember clearly was looking out of the guest room window onto the street hours after the party had been shut down. And there at the only table left, smack in the middle of the pavement, was my father. He sat drunk, slouched in his seat, yelling as the cars swerved by him down the now unobstructed street. I prayed that he didn't get hurt and then I watched my stepmother rock the baby back to sleep.

Over the years my father's wife would attempt to enforce a number of rules when it came to his drinking but none seemed to make much difference. They all varied in futility and ridiculousness. She would take away his weekday beer privileges or roll her eyes a little harder when he reached for his fifth but if they ever truly fought about it I wasn't privy. It is my understanding though that once when my father took things too far and passed out at a family gathering, my stepmother approached his siblings for help. They laughed her off much the same way that my father had laughed at me years earlier. It was not something that was meant to be questioned or discussed and that just had to be understood.

I called my father up last year to wish him a happy birthday. The day was almost done and it was clear from the moment that he answered the phone that he was hammered. I thought maybe he had gone out for some libations with the boys but he told me, in slurred shouts, that he hadn't gone anywhere at all. Instead, he said, my younger sister had prepared dinner for him and they all had enjoyed a quiet night in. In an instant I felt sad for my sisters and then, in a much different way, for him.

I don't know if my father is an alcoholic but I do know that he has made his drinking a problem for us all.

twelve.

It is one sort of an emotional burden on a child of divorce when they are left to believe that they are not as important to their parent as the new children in their new family might be. It is a whole other sort of burden when they are all but told as much.

I remember clearly how it felt the first time that I was given that message.

It was an October and I was thirteen. I was sitting downstairs on my mother's new couch, all dressed up and ready to go with my coat in my lap but my father was already late to pick me up. It was the day of my younger cousin's birthday party and I had had it marked in big blue ink on the calendar in my bedroom for weeks. Next to me on the floor sat the present for him that I had bought with my own money and wrapped to the best of my somewhat lacking craft abilities. I can't recall now just what it was but I know that I was beaming with pride to give it to him. I tapped my foot impatiently as I glanced out the window again and again anxiously awaiting the arrival of my father's car.

But instead of a car's engine I heard a ringing phone. The caller ID lit up with my father's mobile number and I snatched the receiver to me in a hurry.

He wasn't coming.

He talked quickly and he sugarcoated nothing. He told me that the baby was being fussy in the car and he just didn't think it was worth the extra bit of driving that it would require to take me along with them to the party. They were going to go without me.

I was crushed, but as was all too common in such frequent instances of disappointment, I said nothing of my hurting to my father. Through trembling lips I told him that I understood. Then I hung up the phone and went to find my mother upstairs so that I could cry properly about being so abruptly kicked off the invite list. Through tears and hiccups I told her about the change in plans. I told her what my father had said about how he couldn't come get me because he thought it might upset the baby and my mother watched as her own baby struggled not to be devastated.

I don't know what it must be like for one parent to watch, helpless, as their child is continually hurt by the other parent. I imagine it cannot feel good to realize that half of the time the person that you must protect them from is the one person who was supposed to be protecting them right alongside you.

Then, always a stickler for manners and maybe just to make sure that my father had some consequences for his actions, my mother headed to the telephone. She called my uncle and told him that I would not be in attendance at his son's party and then she told him just why. It was not even ten minutes later that my father rang again to say that he would, in fact, be coming to get me. It seemed my godfather, and always the favorite uncle, was not one to hold back with my father in the way that I was. The situation was remedied and I got to attend the party as planned. But I don't remember the party, I don't remember what was in the gift wrap that I carried along with me, and I don't remember what kind of cake we had there. What I remember is the way my father treated me that day. What I remember is the way that it hurt and how truly unimportant it made me feel. And not for the last time.

There were smaller instances of similar interactions as the years went on. My father would miscount his children in front of me when a neighbor asked (*"I've got two—oh, three girls"*) or refer to my sisters as "his kids" when conversing with me. Each thoughtless moment tore a stitch out of a wound desperate to heal. But none more so than an incident on a rainy night in March when I was just shy of nineteen.

My mother and most of the rest of our immediate

family had relocated to Florida shortly after my high school graduation. My birthday fell over my school's spring break that year and I was heading down to the Sunshine State to ring in the coming of another year of life. I had spent the night prior to my flight sleeping at my father's house so that he could drive me to the airport the next day. He lived just a short drive away from it, maybe fifteen minutes or so, and he was able to deliver me easily and with time to spare on the evening of my scheduled departure.

Scheduled being the key word. The flight got delayed. First it was just an hour, and then they added another. Then they boarded us onto the plane and then they took us off the plane. Then they delayed it again once more for good measure before they went ahead and cancelled the damn thing all together. Anyone with a ticket for that flight would have to wait until morning to see the friendly skies. The weather was just fine there in Newark but a mechanical problem meant the plane wasn't leaving the ground anytime that night. I called my family in Florida who scurried to see if there was another flight I could be booked on that was leaving that night and I inquired about the same at the airport. It was no use. I was looking at at least a twelve-hour stint in a plastic chair at Newark Liberty International. I called my father to ask him to come get me. It wasn't very late, maybe a bit before nine, and the idea of being alone there for all those hours with all those strangers was unsettling to my teenage self. I was surprised when he told me that no, he would not come to rescue me. He empathized with my travel frustration for a moment but said that my sisters were already in their beds and my stepmother was not at home. I was slightly stunned. He was just going to leave his teenage daughter alone overnight at the airport because he couldn't ask a neighbor to sit with my sisters for fifteen minutes? He couldn't put them in coats and throw them in the car for a quick trip? When I think about it now, even the offer of cab fare would have made all the difference. I hung up the phone and sat alone for hour after hour as I watched the airport shut down around me. I thought back to that birthday party a few years earlier but this time I didn't cry. The feeling of disappointment had grown too familiar. Second best felt commonplace now and the sting of the hurt was duller this time. And to me, that was the saddest thing of all.

thirteen.

I do not like money. When I have it and especially when I do not, I find money to be just a source of endless aggravation and unneeded stress. It makes me uncomfortable. I do not like discussing it with strangers and I certainly do not like discussing it with friends or family. I am very content to keep my finances between me, my bank teller and the craps dealer at my local casino. That being said, just to call my father "cheap" would fall short of the lengthy explanation that such a worthy accusation deserves.

When the ruling came down on the child support required of my father it was, as such things tend to be, based on his salary at the time. My father would switch jobs several times after that over the years but my mother never asked the court to reevaluate the payments. Perhaps her decision was prideful and misguided but my father never attempted to contribute additional monies elsewhere. I have never received any items from my father that were not birthday gifts or Christmas presents. He never bought me a pair of sneakers or a winter coat. He never chipped in for school supplies or incidentals. When I was in high school and was strapped for the extra cash necessary to participate in the freshman basketball season I approached him cautiously to ask for the funds. He said he'd contribute half of the requested amount and only if my mother paid the other half.

Each time he changed jobs, as he was apt to do for quite a stretch, it would delay the child support payments for weeks as each new human resources department passed the paperwork from one inbox to another. Health insurance was no different. Coverage would lapse each time my father fancied a new employer. I, of course, was not privy to this information as a child and I only share it with you now so that you can better understand this next bit of charming discourse.

Academics were not my strong suit. I excelled in English but just the idea of cracking open a math book could make my head spin. I got an A on every essay I wrote in high school but I took Earth Science twice. I was restless and my focus was elsewhere. The idea of devoting four years of my life to a college to earn a degree I didn't want seemed counterproductive to every other goal I had in my mind for myself. It also seemed like a waste of money.

I wanted to be a performer and I wanted to be a

writer. I am, by the way, both of those things today and I'm doing just fine but at the time my father thought the very idea of such pursuits was pointless. I am not discounting the value of a college education but I don't think it's for everyone and I knew it was not for me.

I had big dreams of the Big Apple. My best friend and I would talk for hours about how we were going to pack our bags and move to New York City the minute after they gave us our diplomas. I was hell bent on seeing my dream come true but I was an excited eighteen and my mother was far more rational about the whole thing. She told me that the only way I was moving anywhere was if I was going to school. It didn't have to be a four-year institution, but I had to be somewhere learning something and preferably living in a dorm. I did my best to compromise. After months of research I found an acting conservatory in the city that seemed like heaven to me. The work would be hard, full eight-hour days five days a week and more classes on Saturdays but the faculty was incredible and the course load seemed inspiring. Completion of the two year program would leave me with transferable college credits that were equivalent to an Associate's degree should I have decided that perhaps attending a four-year school was something that seemed remotely interesting to me.

My father, who had never shown any interest at all in my scholastic endeavors, was suddenly fully invested in my post-graduation plans. This, of course, had nothing to do with my well-being and everything to do with the divorce agreement stating that he was required to participate financially in my higher education. He even accompanied my mother and me on the tour of the school in the winter of my senior year but he asked nothing of our guide and instead chose to hang back and make snide comments under his breath for the duration of the tour. He had his mind made up about my choice long before we ever stepped off the train.

The Judgement of Divorce stated clearly in black and white:

> *"The parties and the minor child shall discuss the choice of college and mutually make a decision regarding same."*

If he didn't agree with my mother and me then I imagine, it seemed to him, that he would not have to contribute to the decision financially. He refused to help at all. He would even go so far as to not provide the information necessary for me to fill out my loan paperwork in a timely fashion. He was stubborn about the idea and would only talk to me in caustic tones about it all.

My father can be a cruel and cutting man but never more so than when I called to tell him in the spring of the following year that I had been accepted to the school. Months had passed between the tour and the good news letter arriving and my father had not yet said much about his refusal to help so the way he spoke to me on the phone that day caught me off guard and stung all that much harder. He ridiculed me, he cursed, he called me an "idiot" and the school "a joke." He hung up on me and I broke down crying like a child on the kitchen floor.

That is what I remember most about the day that I got into the school of my dreams. My family around me, champagne glasses half full from our toast to the news, and me on the floor in tears with my father's voice looping through my head. My acceptance letter was still in my hand.

I do not remember much about the chain of events between that March and June, but I know that I was not allowed to stay hurt for long. My father attended my graduation and his whole family came to the party that my mother held for me in a cousin's backyard. But he and I, we didn't talk much. In July he filed the formal court papers that he hoped would absolve him of his financial obligation.

Now not only was my mother trying to help to put me through school but she was racking up a debt of lawyer fees and the guilt was becoming too much for me to bear. I wasn't angry at my father because he would not pay for my education; I was angry because he had treated me so harshly and because in refusing to help me he had once again managed to punish my mother.

I didn't talk to him for months. One night he left me a voicemail telling me that it made him ill that I had only used him for money. What money?! It would have been funny if it hadn't been so hurtful. I never cared about the money. I cared about the way he talked to me. I cared about the way he disregarded what I wanted. I cared about the words he had used and the way he left me crying on the kitchen floor.

A month into my first semester, his wife called me at school. It was my father's birthday and against my better judgment, I answered the phone. She spent the first few minutes stuttering through small talk and then let the barely constructed facade fall away. Soon she was all but begging me to please call my father. She went on and on telling me about how he had been moping around the house all day and how she thought it would mean so much to him if I just picked up the phone and told him happy birthday. So I did. I called him and I played nice and I wished him well. Because try as I might I could never be the kind of person my father was. I could never knowingly hurt someone the way he could. So I pushed aside my feelings and I swallowed my pride, all for the sake of making him feel better. My father may have turned another year older that day but I was once again left feeling like the adult.

In the end, without his help, I was only able to afford two semesters at the school. The week that I left, my father emancipated me because I was no longer a full time student. He stripped me of the right to be on his health insurance two whole years before the law would have. It was ironic because I had never felt sicker about the whole thing.

fourteen.

I was born and raised, and for most of my life have lived, in the great state of New Jersey and because of that it is just an undeniable fact that I will always love Bruce Springsteen more than you can. Unless, of course, you were also born and raised in New Jersey in which case, let us join together for a rousing chorus of "Bruuuuce!" over shots at The Stone Pony.

For many, music from the leader of the E Street band conjures up thoughts of fast cars and freedom. And while they may hear Bruce as an anthem for taking the wheel, to me, he has always been the soundtrack of the passenger seat.

On the weekend drives up and down the Garden State Parkway from my house to my father's and back again it was comfortingly common for the car to be filled with the sounds of The Boss. And for the first few years, I listened obviously and intently. I was much too young then to understand what most of the songs were saying but it didn't matter. I loved them because my father did. But with age came attitude. Soon I thought that adolescence was no time to be enjoying the same music as my ancient dad so I donned my headphones and rolled my eyes every time that he pressed "play." I would drown out the sounds of John Hiatt and Joe Cocker with boy bands and pop stars but I would always pause that noise for Bruce. Oh, I never took the earpieces off or gave any indication at all that I was listening, but I was. Just as intently as I ever had been, but never again as obviously. To this day when I hear Springsteen songs, I am transported. With just a few chords I am once again a child, sitting in the passenger seat of my dad's car as we fly past mile markers and exit signs.

One day after adolescence had given way to adulthood and most of my bad taste had been replaced by better music, I let my father in on my well-kept secret. I was a Bruce Springsteen fan, too. More than that, I always had been. He laughed when I told him how I would stop my Walkman when I heard the start of "Thunder Road" and he smiled when I said that I had seen Bruce and the band in concert for the first time that summer that we weren't speaking. I teared up when they played all the songs that reminded me of my father's car but I didn't tell him that part.

About a year or so later, my dad relayed a story to me in passing, just a throwaway anecdote that he thought was entertaining. He said that he had recently taken my sister to see Springsteen and he told me how amazing that had been for him. He said he even cried a little just watching her there. His voice took on a special sentimental tone and it hurt me to hear him talk. And then it hurt me even harder when he said that my sister had brought along a friend to the show that night ... because he'd had an extra ticket.

Maybe it was silly and selfish but I felt slighted. I had never even crossed his mind. I thought about what it might have been like to have shared that experience with my father. I thought about what it might have been like to have really been back in that passenger seat one more time.

It occurred to me not that long ago that perhaps I had never properly shown my father what that music meant to me. Maybe I have never truly thanked him for the introduction. That was why I was so excited last year when I had the opportunity to guest deejay on a satellite radio station that was entirely Springsteen themed. I was asked to pick out five songs to play on the air and I thought long and hard about each choice before I made my selections. I wanted to play my personal favorites but I also wanted to be sure to include the ones that had such strong nostalgic value to me. I wanted it to be a gesture to my dad. I wanted him to know how much I valued those songs and what they represented to me.

I went to visit him not long after my list had been made but before the show was to air and I told him enthusiastically about the upcoming event. Before I could proudly rattle off the playlist that I had picked, he stopped me. He said he couldn't believe that I hadn't consulted with him first and I laughed because his tone seemed jovial. Then he said, in a less good-natured voice, that it was just one more thing to add to the list of times I had disappointed him.

Suddenly I didn't care about the songs or the station or even, excuse me fellow New Jerseyians, Springsteen. My mind was reeling backwards.

It was hurtful and so blatantly uncalled for in that moment. I laughed again because I didn't know what else to do. Perhaps he had been joking about the importance of consulting him but there was no humor in his voice when he said the rest.

When I arrived home that evening I emailed the radio station to change my selections. I pulled some tracks that I had wanted to play off the list to accommodate the ones my father had asked for because I didn't want to let him down again. My good intentions for a heartfelt tribute had become, instead, a heartbreaking endeavor and those new songs were now its soundtrack.

fifteen.

When I was nineteen years old I was crashing on my best friend's pull-out couch in New York City and balancing multiple odd jobs to try and make ends meet. I had left school but I didn't want to leave the city. There was nothing for me in Florida where my mother was and my father had made it clear that staying at his house for any extended period of time was not an option. So I was living exactly in the position that I had been aiming for at seventeen. Turns out that my mom had been right and it was tougher than I had thought it would be. I missed school and I missed my family. I also missed eating anything that hadn't been covered in plastic wrap and stamped with the word Ramen.

One month when finances were particularly tough, I accepted my father's offer to babysit the girls for a week while they were on a break from school. It so happened that at the time my cell phone bill was a bit past due and the company was threatening to shut it off. I was up-front about my troubles and asked my father if I could have half of the money just a few days in advance so that I could pay my bill. He told me no. He said that he was afraid that if he gave me the money early I wouldn't show up to watch my sisters. In an instant I didn't care about the cash or my phone. He was treating me like some kind of sneaky thief. He thought I was going to steal from him?! I had never done anything in my life to give my father the impression that I would ever do a thing like that but it didn't matter. It was just another startling reminder that he had always been so distrusting of me. My paranoid father was constantly inventing motives for my behavior in his mind. It was infuriating and hurtful. More than that, it was misdirected. Once again my father had managed to misfire his long-held doubts about my mother's truth-telling and he was hitting me square in the gut.

I wanted to cancel on the job right then and there. I didn't even want his money anymore. But the bills were piling up and principles were expensive so I didn't say another word. When I look back now I have no idea how much I was paid or where I allocated the funds but I remember every bit of suspicion in my father's voice when he told me he didn't trust me. I have never forgotten the way it made me feel so incredibly small.

sixteen.

My father did help me once. It was a grand gesture and so it was very unlike him. Maybe you even heard him tell the story somewhere. He would do it at the drop of a dime and he loved to work it into each and every available opening that he saw. Regardless of the wedging it required. I quickly found myself growing less and less grateful with each "thank you" that the tellings demanded.

With my short-lived shot at higher education come and gone and my bank account dwindling I knew that it was time to make some changes and set some goals. So I moved back to New Jersey and settled in with my aunt and uncle while I worked through the summer at a liquor store they owned in my home-town. They were generous and I was appreciative. In a few months time I had saved up enough money that I could make a move so I made a big one. I found an apartment and an internship in Nashville, Tennessee and just like that I had a new plan. The cost of living was cheaper down there and the music was better. It would do until I could figure out my next course of action.

My mother and I loaded up her car and together we drove the thirteen-and-a-half hours to my new home down in Dixie. She stuck around for a day or two and then took the long drive back on her own while I adjusted to my new surroundings.

Each day was a new adventure and experience in independent living, and I came to truly value my time there. But as the internship wound down and the next chapter of my life started to come into view I realized I could not stay on my Southern detour forever. The novelty of escaping had worn off and it was time to start my real career back up north. I delayed my leaving as long as I could but soon I had to take my restlessness and head home.

I was not yet twenty and I definitely was not twenty-five so renting a car or a U-Haul truck was out of the question. I would need the assistance of someone else to make the trip. My mother was living in Florida at the time and my father was my only option. I was relieved and frankly, surprised when he begrudgingly agreed to fly down and rent a vehicle so that we could drive me and my various belongings back up to New Jersey. Hear me when I say now that I was full of gratitude. I understand that it was not my parents' obligation to move me each time my fickle young mind decided it was ready to get up and get gone and I thanked my father profusely. But if I had known then that he would bring it up in the years to follow even half as much as he actually did I would have walked home.

The man has never once missed an opportunity to make a cutting jab about the time he had to sweep in and save me. I have heard the story retold to anyone who will listen time and time again with the drive getting longer and longer in each rendition.

I suppose that every time he tells the story he hopes that I will once again be reminded of my gratitude and in truth, I am. Though I assume it is not the reminder he intends. Because while I do find myself full of thankfulness it is not for him but for my mother. To her that move was just one more act of maternal love. It was no different than all the times she stayed up with me at night to watch my fever or drove me to school when I missed the bus. It was just one small act among millions. I understand now why my father had to make such a big deal out of that particular story. It was the only one he had.

seventeen.

"Go ahead, act something. You want to be an actor?
Act right here."

That was the hook of a familiar medley of taunts
that my father would sing out at various holiday
gatherings. My dad always needed to be the center of
attention and it didn't matter at whose expense. It was
a reoccurring theme for all of my life. I would laugh
uncomfortably or roll my eyes until my grandmother
inevitably reprimanded her oldest, and most immature, son to close his mouth and try to play nice.

My father just did not know how to do supportive
and on some level, I accepted that. I realized early in
life that my ambitions were not always going to be the
kind that were met with the most serious of consider-
ation from my family. Even though my dad had played
in various bands for as long as I could remember and

harbored dreams of being a voice-over actor, such things seemed silly and unattainable since he, himself, had never attained them. I didn't pay much mind to his teasing until around the time that it stopped.

It was a Christmas Eve afternoon and my father's family had assembled at my aunt's house to celebrate. We exchanged pleasantries and bits of small talk until my father once again took over the room. But this year he didn't want to mock me about my dramatic prowess, he wanted to clear the way for my baby sister to boast about hers. It seems that not only did my dad fully support my sister's new found dreams of stage and screen, he was a willing and active participant in trying to make them come true.

He smiled and laughed as together they told the story of how just a few weeks prior they had camped out together on the streets of New York so that my sister could attend an open casting call for The Lion King on Broadway. Then my father started to go on and on about different acting classes they were looking into and the varying prices of the programs.

I found myself doing some mental calculations and wondering if I could have afforded another semester at school if he had been as open to giving half of that to my own ambitions. Ya know, the ones that I was working tirelessly on before I found out that there already was a star in the family.

In truth, I was happy to find out that I shared my passion for the arts with my sister. She is a talented kid. I was relieved that my father had chosen to encourage her and that she would not be subjected to the same public mocking that I had been for all those years. But I would be lying if I said that I didn't feel like once again, I had somehow missed the (show)boat.

eighteen.

I was born on March 29th. My dad still, from time to time, makes reference to the number twenty-nine in a variety of ways. He's had email addresses that ended in it or fantasy baseball teams that have somehow incorporated it and I always appreciated the small nod. Because birthdays are serious business.

I don't remember when it was exactly that my dad and I stopped celebrating mine together. When I was very young, and if my birthday happened to fall near my father's weekend, he would sometimes throw a small party for me at his home. It was fun and thoughtful and very short lived.

Some years later, when I was old enough to drive, my father would ask me if I wanted to come up and see him for my birthday. Each year I would explain that it wasn't very much fun for me to drive an hour each way and that it was my day after all. He always agreed and promised that he would instead make the ride down and take me out to dinner. But he never once showed up.

On my twenty-fifth birthday, he sent a text message. His mother, his brothers and his sisters all managed to call but my dad could not be bothered to do the same. It made me sad and that made me angry. At myself. I hated that such seemingly trivial things could impact me so instantaneously when he was involved.

When it was one of my sisters' birthdays I always made the effort to be there for whatever sort of celebrations were going on. If my weekend work plans conflicted with a scheduled party I would make the drive on the actual date instead and join in on their birthday dinner. It was important for me to stay active in the tradition that I had started and I knew it meant something to them.

The older turned sixteen in January of 2011. A sweet sixteen party is pretty big news but I hadn't heard anything at all about one from my dad so I sent him an email a few days before her birthday. I asked him if they hadn't planned out a party and if I should, instead, just come up during the week. My father wrote back a few hours later to tell me that they were in fact having quite the celebration. He just hadn't remembered to tell me. I was a little put off but I tried to take it in stride. I was doing okay until I found out that actual, physical invitations had been mailed to everyone else in his family.

He didn't just forget to tell me, he forgot to invite me. If I had said nothing would I ever even have known about the party? I was livid and for once I didn't bite my tongue.

I asked my father if there was any reason in particular that my name had been left off the mailing list. I heard nothing back from him for days and then I received a reply from his wife. It was an apology for my father's oversight. I fumed. Now not only was I not deemed worth of an invitation but he was having someone else handle his apologies.

With such lacking correspondence skills I wondered how he had even managed to write me off at all.

nineteen.

My father told me once that he worried that he had perhaps not been the best dad because he hadn't had the best example. He was thirteen when his father left and I suppose he thought it seemed like suitable cause for a lack of paternal instinct. To me it always sounded like a cop-out. My father has two brothers, both younger, who were excellent fathers from the instant that their children were born. Just as my father was. Only his brothers never wavered in their responsibilities in the way that he did.

I believe that the difference has everything to do with priority and nothing to do with paternity.

When I was very young and up until my parents got divorced, my father was an excellent parent because I was a priority in his life. Not only was I his daughter but I was the daughter of his wife. I was an integral and important part of his family unit. But when that unit was divided and he chose to seek another, his priorities shifted.

In fits of generosity sometimes I wonder if perhaps my father wasn't so much a bad dad as he was a lackluster multi-tasker. But in either case, it seems he thought he had fixed the problem.

A few months back before the break-up I was chatting with one of my sisters when she let it slip how excited she was about the new children that would be coming to stay with her and her family. My mind was racing but she supplied the information before I even had time to ask the question. They were becoming a foster family.

Do you have any idea what it's like to find out that the man who couldn't be bothered to parent you thinks he's so god damn good at it now that he's volunteering to do it for kids that aren't even his?

I was shocked to say the least but I did my best to keep the surprise out of my features while my sister rambled on excitedly. And though I could appreciate the good deed that was being done, the absurdity of it all was enough to make me laugh right out loud.

My father was taking care of children whose parents had abandoned them. In a rush my mind filled with what I knew but had not yet said and suddenly it wasn't so funny anymore.

twenty.

I was three months into eighteen when I felt the earth shake. I remember the moment with perfect clarity. I know for sure the way the carpet felt under me as I lay stretched out on the floor and I can still recall with precision just the way the keyboard felt under my fingertips when my hands froze against it. It was the summer after my high school graduation and I was sure that I was now an adult ready to face the world and everyone in it. But I could never have imagined just who I would come to encounter.

It was early evening when I, without permission but with great curiosity, logged into my mother's email account. My parents had been fighting for months over my father's insistence that he would not help pay for my continued education and my mother was only relaying bits and pieces of the dispute back to me. Unsatisfied with the limited information I began to dig deeper on my own. I could not have known or even possibly imagined the magnitude of what I would discover among their communication and the way it would go on to affect me.

Typed out just before the closing of an email from my mother to my father was a biting line. She had written to him that she would not let me be forgotten in the same way that he had forgotten about his other child. *Other child?!* My eyes read the text over and over again trying to make sense of it. Questions stampeded through my mind. Had my parents had another baby together before I came along? It seemed unlikely. My maternal grandmother surely would have let that slip out a time or two over the years. So that meant that my dad had sired another child somewhere along the way. When? Was it while my parents were married? Where was this child now? I was immediately torn between the need to know more and the fear of what emotions knowing could bring.

I didn't say a word to anyone for a few days while I tried to process the implications of my new discovery. It didn't help that I had come across the information in a less than honorable way. I knew my mother was not going to be thrilled to find out I'd gone exploring in her inbox. After some time had passed I told my new-found secret to a friend. He asked more questions that I didn't have the answers to and eventually my curiosity stood in for courage and I approached my mother. I was thankful that the weight of the subject matter took precedence over the shady way in which I had acquired the information. I may have used my mother's computer illiteracy and my strong storytelling abilities to brush over the inconsequential details of the find. Either way, I made my mouth release the words that had been rattling around in my brain for nearly a week:

"Did Dad have a kid before me?"

I don't know what I expected. Maybe denial at the allegation or some shock at the unveiling of my excavated information. But my mother's reaction was passive at best. She gave no hint that my inquiry was unexpected. I suppose she always knew that some day I could stumble upon this well-kept secret and so she confirmed it without missing a beat. My heart filled my throat and my gut caved in as I listened to the limited details she was able to offer. My father had had a son not long before I was born. I was told that he denied paternity until the baby was born and a test proved otherwise. To my mother's knowledge he only ever saw his child once—in a courtroom. A few years later my father signed away his rights to the biological mother's new husband and just like that it was over. He walked away from an unwanted situation and in doing so he walked away from his child. I could only see in this story, a foreshadowing of my own. Would my father have signed away his rights to me if it had been an option? Is that the kind of man he was? I was uncomfortable with the emotions and implications I found myself sifting through under the weight of this discovery.

Time went on as time tends to do until the days became years and I seldom thought about my father's firstborn. It was all vague and intangible, barely more than a hypothetical. Until one night when it grew to be so real that it forever changed my reality.

Because success in my chosen field often requires that people who I don't know, do know me, I occasionally find myself interacting with strangers on popular social networking sites. I never thought much about the possibilities of those connections until one night when I received a message from someone who claimed to be my brother.

It was late, maybe almost four in the morning when he contacted me. He wasted no time in getting to the point. First a warning that the interaction may be awkward and then "I think we're brother and sister" came across my screen. I immediately started flipping through his online photo albums but even now I'm not sure what I was hoping to find. He didn't look much like my father. Maybe a bit like my uncle if I squinted. Was this just some comedy fan with a twisted sense of humor? I formed the only question I could and asked him what my father's name was. He answered correctly right away. Well, that didn't mean anything at all. Anyone who knows me could know that. I was all out of inquires that would offer up any proof that would satisfy me. I didn't know enough about the situation to request the necessary information. I looked twice at the clock before I decided there was only one thing I could do. I phoned my mother.

At the time I was out on tour with some other comics, a few states from home and I'm sure a ringing cellular in the middle of the night scared the woman half to death. It took me several moments to assure her that I was fine maybe because I didn't know for certain that I was. I quickly told her what had happened and asked her what I could ask of this stranger to know if he was in fact, my family. She still remembered the name of his mother, as I imagine you always do in that sort of situation, so I hurried back to my computer to seek the confirmation I feared attaining. And there, with just a few keystrokes in the dim light of my laptop screen, I had a brother.

He was a soldier in the US Army and a veteran of the war in Iraq. Just a year older than I was and an alum of a high school in my hometown. Further inspection of his pictures showed him grinning with a friend of mine. It was surreal. I asked him if he had ever met our father and he said that he had not. He recalled a time when he was eight and had asked his mother about a possible meeting and she warned him that my dad might not be receptive to the idea. Just like that any want the young boy had had for a connection was gone. He confessed though that he had tried to reach out again via the same social networking site a few months earlier while stationed overseas but had never gotten a reply. I felt dizzy with emotion. The pit in my stomach swelled. I felt an innate urge to defend my father and then felt sick with myself at the impulse. How could a man who watched his own father walk out then himself turn and leave his son behind? Did he ever think about him? How could he receive a message from his flesh and blood stationed in a war zone and never return contact? The questions spun around my mind and echoed in the emptiness that the lack of answers supplied.

In talking to my brother, intangible pieces of the story suddenly started to feel heavy on my heart. I was already born, nearly four years old, the day that my father signed away his son. I could not then, nor can I still now, comprehend how he could differentiate his attachment to one child from another. What made that boy any less of his child than I was? Was it only because he happened to be married to my mother? That would prove to be temporary. Was I as disposable to him as his eldest was? Suddenly it was hard to breathe.

Every excuse that I had allowed myself to afford my father over the years fell away in an instant. I was not his first child. I was not his first misstep as a parent. I was his first chance to do better and he had fallen short again. I had believed for years that my sisters were simply reaping the benefits of my father's second chance. I had never truly realized until that moment that it was, in fact, me and not them who should have been his redemption.

There comes a moment when every child looks at their parent and sees them not as an infallible idol or an out-of-touch antique but instead as a person capable of a great range of sin and indiscretions. It is the time when we first understand that regardless of age or familial hierarchy we are truly nothing more than peers coexisting in the world. When relationships are stripped of nostalgia and obligation, all that is left is the emotion that the connection invokes and the respect on which it survives. I had lost that respect for my father and in doing so the only emotion I could feel was grief.

I felt strange in the company of all the new information I had discovered. My emotions varied on a day-to-day basis as I tried to come to terms with what it all meant.

From the time that my sisters had been born I was taught to treat them just as I would have full-blooded siblings even though we only shared one biological parent. Why should it be any different with this new-found brother? It was all the same thing. Had that thought ever crossed my father's mind when he saw all of his daughters together?

I wondered little things like if my dad remembered his son's birthday every year or if he didn't even know what day it was. How removed had he let himself become?

I was torn between the desire to know this mystery sibling and the feeling that in doing so I would somehow betray my father. More than once I made plans to meet him and then abruptly cancelled when my nerves grew to be too great. I found myself angry at my father for giving me yet another emotional cross to bear.

I knew that I had to say something but despite my best efforts I just couldn't get the words to fit together right. I started so many emails but not one got sent. They all seemed so pointless. I had no questions to ask of my father and I wasn't waiting for any explanations or apologies. I wanted only to tell him what I knew and about how my respect for him had fallen away under the weight of the information. But I couldn't bring myself to say it. Ironically, it still seemed too disrespectful.

twenty-one.

On May 30th of 2010 my grandmother, my mother's mother, passed away after a short but brutally trying battle with cancer. It is without exaggeration that I say that losing her was the single greatest pain that I had ever known. I do not think that there are enough words in the world that I could use to properly express the immense sadness that I felt in the wake of her death. To put it much too simply, I was shattered.

For all of its changing definitions over the years, my grandmother was always at the core of what I believed the word family meant. She was an active, intricately involved part of my life and every day that I lived it. I was crushed under the thought that I would have to live the rest of my life without her.

My father had never been shy about voicing his dislike for my grandmother and it had, over the years, made me increasingly uncomfortable. On more than one occasion he had called her "crazy" and it made me cringe.

Now, I will not make the woman a saint just because she's dead. She was at times borderline unbearable. She was judgmental and stubborn and oh so opinionated. But she was my Nanny and I loved her. She had stepped in when my father walked out and I always believed that she deserved more respect for that than he ever showed her.

On the day of the funeral, I was touched to see my dad and most of his family in attendance. He had rallied the troops for me and they came out in full support. His efforts and their presence meant so much to me and I was truly grateful. I thought that maybe, if nothing else, he had come to understand how invaluable she was to his daughter's life. And perhaps through loving and respecting me, he had come to respect her.

But I was wrong. My father did not respect me or the bond my grandmother and I shared at all. And he wasted almost no time in showing me that.

One day while on the Internet I took some time to casually stalk my sister's social networking profile the way that one does on those sorts of sites. Her page was public and I worried that perhaps the same long lost brother that found me would consider reaching out to her, too. I figured that if I said nothing else I should at least tell my father that his sixteen-year-old daughter's page should not be open for the world to see. But before I could do anything else, a small thumbnail sized picture of him caught my eye on the left hand side of the screen. I clicked the link and his networking page unfolded into my browser. It just took one quick glance and I could feel my blood boil.

Written across the top of my father's status for the day was a poorly conceived, off-color joke about my greatly missed grandmother. I saw red and my head pounded twice as loud as my heart. That bastard. The joke wasn't even funny. I'm a stand-up comedian. I would have cut him a little slack if the punchline was worth the punch to my gut but it just wasn't. Together in the comments section he and a friend of his laughed over my grandmother now being his "ex-ex mother-in-law." Get it? 'Cause she's dead. The only thing more offensive than him posting the joke was how bad of a joke it was.

My hands shook as I clicked the browser over to my email account and I started stabbing at the keys. It was the first time in my life that I didn't hold back my emotions from my father. I poured them out across the keyboard and I hit send.

I told him that his status was unnecessary and offensive. I told him that it was hurtful and disrespectful to me. Regardless of his relationship with his ex-wife I was his current daughter and I was still in pain daily over the loss of my grandmother.

Across the bottom of the email I pounded out an angry after thought. It was the only weapon I had with which to stab back. I told him right there in black and white that he should take my sister's profile off its public setting because I was recently contacted by his illegitimate son through that website and it was a shitty way to find out something that I would rather not know.

And just like that it was over. It felt done. After all those years and all those disappointments it had all come down to one undeniable, irreversible truth.

I did not respect my father, and his actions that day showed me that he did not respect me. And without respect, we had nothing.

It was simple and it was sad and it was over.

twenty-two.

I am a perpetual reader, a bit of a writer, and a fairly conspicuous word nerd. Definitions fascinate me and I have always found a certain level of dork joy in expanding my vocabulary. I tell you this so that you may better understand me when I tell you that I am not sure that I have ever truly comprehended the meaning of the word "forgive."

Webster tells me that as a transitive verb it means "*to cease to feel resentment against an offender*" and while my critical mind digests that with ease, my emotions do wander. If my fingers take to wandering as well then I find myself in the "R" section of the dictionary and there I could read the following:

Resentment (noun) *Bitter indignation at having been treated unfairly*

And so continues my inner turmoil. I do not feel bitter. I have been angry but more often I have been hurt. I have not consciously tried to maintain negative feelings where my father is concerned but they have attached themselves to memories and moments that I cannot shake. Such is the danger in bruising a child. These small upsets that occur in the early years of life are not simply dents in an already constructed wall; worse yet, they are the cracks created in the foundation.

Once on an episode of Oprah someone said that forgiveness meant *"giving up the hope that the past could have been any different."* That's a bit more abstract and I stumble with all that it suggests. I do not wish that the past could have been different. I am who I am because of it. I only mean to correct the present and not drag it into the future. And in that way I feel like it could be said that I have forgiven my father. But in truth, I guess I just don't understand what is mine to absolve him of.

I cannot change how his actions made me feel and though I remember the past I do not hold tight to those emotions today. They are simply etched there, intricately wound around each moment in my memory. Just as happiness is tied to lighter recollections.

But I am not willing to create any new memories. That is what this break-up means. It's an eternal pause button. It's as though I am saying we will stop here, with just the moments we have already acquired, and that's it. We will create nothing new together. Because I am not willing to risk having even one more permanent etching that only brings me sadness.

I am not so naive as to think that I am not at all to blame for the issues that exist between me and my father. I know that I have been guilty of blindly setting expectations that perhaps I never properly articulated to him. I know now, as an adult, that I cannot be angry because someone failed to meet my idea of who they should be. My father is a flawed and complicated human being just as I am, just as we all are. I know this because reason and logic tell me so. But this wisdom that has infiltrated my mind over the years is a stranger to my heart. My heart does not learn, it adjusts. It has bent under the weight of hope and it has sank with great loss. It has pounded through anxiety and shrank with disappointment. My heart has shattered with the impact of cold words and it has burned with the anger of righteous indignation. But through it all it has kept its beat through every break.

Neither the world nor the people in it can match the ideal version you create in your mind. No one out there is going to be exactly who you want them to be. And that's just not something that you can get mad about. I have tried to remind myself of this fact over and over again throughout the years. I sought comfort in the idea that perhaps my father's shortcomings were just products of my own misguided longings but each time I saw him exceed my expectations when in the company of his other children, that attempt at comfort failed to soothe me. So I learned that I had to look away. And when my father once again tread too heavily on my fragile heart I learned that I had to walk away.

I will love my father for all my life. I will do it in the same way that I always have. From a distance. But this time it will be my choice.

the epilogue.

Just as you will close the book on these chapters, so too will I.

I will shut the cover like a door and I will walk away, leaving these stories behind me. But I will be a little wiser for having written them.

This began as a journey in search of answers and I have found them. Some to questions I hadn't even thought to ask. And while the hurting may still find me from time to time I do not plan on leaving a forwarding address.

There is a well known Bible passage that tells the story of the Judgement of Solomon. It says that once in Israel two women came before the king, both were stubborn and insistent, claiming to be the mother of the same baby and so he declared that he would cut the child in two so that each woman could have half. In the end, the real mother cried out that she would rather see the child be without her than split in two.

Whether it be with a sword or a divorce, when you divide a child you leave them in pieces. My only hope is that now my father will just leave me in peace.

the thank yous.

These stories would have gone untold if not for the support of so many generous people. A million thank yous to everyone who believed in this project when it was only just being born. Thank you for taking this incredible ride with me.

A little bit of extra, endless gratitude belongs to: Mark Caramanna, Jon Heffley, Stef Ferrari, Ayelet Blumberg, William Tisherman, Ritch Sublett, Karl Sakas, Samantha Carter, Kristin Marmion, Douglas Michell, Claire Ratliff, Heather Hanlon-Emeka and Vanessa Potter Wool.

And to Jeny Batten, who knew that this was a book long before I did. Coattails, partner.

But most importantly and with all my love, I thank my mother—who, alone, was more parent than any kid could ever need.